ORPHANED FOXES

A true tale of rescue and release

ALEX KLAUSHOFER

First published in 2018 by Hermes Books
Copyright © Alex Klaushofer 2018
The moral right of the author has been asserted.

All rights reserved. No part of this publication may be reproduced, stored in a retrieval system, or transmitted, in any form or by any means, without the prior written permission of the publisher, except in the case of brief excerpts in reviews and articles.

ISBN 978-0-9933236-1-4
Hermes Books
www.alexklaushofer.com

Cover photo by Peter Trimming

AUTHOR'S NOTE

The question of what to call the foxes who feature in this book raised some key issues to do with our relationship with animals. On the one hand, contemporary zoological correctness, with all its cautioning against anthropomorphism, suggested I refrain from giving them names and find some other, impersonal way of identifying them. But since name-giving is central to how humans relate to other living beings, that seemed an impossible thing to ask of both reader and writer. In the end, I settled on a middle course, using descriptive appellations which, like Native American names, capture an important quality of the named one and the way he is seen. Accordingly, the names of the foxes in this account reflect how they appeared to me and sometimes change with the circumstances. For similar reasons, I've also avoided the use of the word 'it' and taken the liberty of ascribing gender.

It's important to note that what follows is a personal account of one person's experience and in no way constitutes a judgement of any particular approach to animal care.

This book is dedicated to animal lovers and volunteers everywhere.

THE LOOK OF A FOX

This story starts in suburban London. One dark night, I was walking home when I heard a rustling coming from a large pampas grass in a garden in the neighbouring street. It was such a pleasantly busy noise, so redolent of enthusiastic, purposeful activity, that my curiosity was piqued: who or what could it be? On impulse, I stopped and addressed the plant in the sweet tone usually reserved for children and pets. Out popped a fox cub, his face and ears cocked as he looked at me enquiringly. It seemed that he too was curious: he sat down on his haunches, his front paws drawn neatly together, and we both took a good long look at each other. Then he went back into the pampas grass and I went on home. But from that moment on, as far as foxes were concerned, I was a changed woman.

Up until then I had regarded foxes as a nuisance, a pest that threatened the hard work of reclaiming my newly-acquired garden from the bramble-ridden state into which it had fallen. I would plant some bulbs in the bare border to find that, overnight, the soil had been churned up and a little holloway tunnelled under the fence. Holes appeared in the delicate new grass, piles of poo in the middle of the lawn I was struggling to cultivate. I boarded up the tunnels, but more gaps appeared. The foxes' main entry point was the corner farthest from the house which adjoined allotments and another semi-wild garden; the ground was littered with an ever-changing selection of scrabbled stones. So, having read that human smells were a good fox deterrent, I left an old T-shirt sprinkled with my pee wrapped around the tree in Fox Corner.

It made no difference: surrounded on three sides by green spaces connected to a patch of local woodland, my garden was an established thoroughfare for the local wildlife. One winter's morning, I woke to find the ground covered in a blanket of snow. Its crystalline surface was broken only by an animal track that criss-crossed the garden in an organised fashion, covering the ground but never repeating the route. Something about the narrowness of the paw prints and the manner of their imprinting suggested both dexterity and speed, while the coverage indicated a thorough approach. I felt a thrill of urbanite fear: the prints came right up the dozen steps that ran up to the kitchen door. Something wild had tried to get into the flat while I slept.

I don't remember the point at which I gave up trying to keep foxes out of the garden and adopted a policy of relaxed co-existence, cultivating the garden to accommodate both humans and animals. But I do remember the exact moment I first set eyes on Little Fox. It was an evening in late spring and I was cooking, back door open, with one eye on the stove and the other on the garden. There, sitting at the bottom of the steps, was a fox cub, blinking up at me. I told him gently that I wasn't sharing my supper and after a while he went away.

After that, he was often in the garden, prospecting along the fence that ran from Fox Corner to the bottom of the kitchen steps, the slightness of his form thrown into relief by his disproportionately big ears. He was obviously looking for insects – the internet told me that foxes were omnivorous – and although the pickings in my bare border must have been thin, he was clearly making a good start at fending for himself. But the tiny cub who one day appeared in his wake was another matter. He tottered as he tried to imitate the snuffling search of his elder and, as he listed sideways into the grass, I saw his ribs.

Within hours I was at the nearest butcher's, asking about cheap cuts of chicken suitable for foxes. 'Arf! Arf!' laughed the butcher, waving a pack of assorted bits of bone and flesh prepared specially for customers like me. 'They've got you now! Shall I put a packet aside for you next week?' Apparently I was joining a network of soft-hearted south Londoners who fed foxes on a regular basis. It was a surprising outcome for someone who didn't want a pet or believe in taming wild animals and would, I decided, be a temporary arrangement. Since the fox had asked for help, I would give it. But I would put out food irregularly to make sure that, while he didn't starve, he had to learn to scavenge.

I never saw Toddling Cub again, but from then on I was a committed fox-feeder. Every couple of days, I left something in Fox Corner: chicken when I'd been to the butcher and leftovers when I hadn't. Eating in a local cafe which served supersized roasts, I asked for a doggie bag and took the surplus meat home for the fox; instead of throwing away the remains of a tub of taramasalata, I'd put it out. The food always disappeared quickly: the tub would be licked clean, and once I watched as the fox carefully collected the pile of bread I'd left, piece by piece, and took it back under the fence to keep for later. The sight reassured me that he was on the way to self-sufficiency.

But Little Fox was after more than just food: he wanted a safe place to be, and company. He made the garden the focal point of his daytime routine, appearing in the middle of the morning and spending the rest of the day coming and going, curling up on the grass for a nap and then disappearing back under the fence. He would re-appear in the early evening and do a thorough check of the border before taking off for what, I assumed, was his night-patrol of the surrounding area. Sometimes, if I was hanging out washing or doing some gardening, I would turn to find him behind me, his fascinated gaze fixed on the drops of water coming from a sweater or the light reflected by the gloss of falling ivy. Then he would retreat to Fox Corner, where he would sit and look at me. Sometimes I would talk to him quietly, some nonsense about it being all right, and he would blink in acknowledgement. As the warmer weather drew me outside at lunchtimes, he would sometimes join me while I ate. I was pleased when one day he slipped under the fence carrying a small, knotted plastic bag in his jaw. He deposited it onto the ground and, while I worked my way through my plateful, he delved into his bag and consumed some of its contents.

Generally I made it a rule not to share food from my plate. But one lunchtime when Little Fox had come to join me, I made an exception and threw him a few chips. After he'd eaten them, he performed a little dance. He leapt into the air, simultaneously spinning and throwing his body so that he landed in a different place. Another jump, and he executed a reverse pirouette. Then he crouched on the ground a few yards from where I was sitting stretched out on the sun lounger. His eyes locked on mine, holding a mix of fear and desire, and he started to creep towards me. I held my breath: I had another rule, kept half-secret from myself: I couldn't attempt to touch the fox but he could, if he chose, get close to me. He continued to creep closer until, ever so gently, he enclosed the toe of my outstretched boot in his mouth. A second or so later he was off again, hurling himself backwards towards the border where he bit off the head of a giant daisy. [1]

By this stage, toys had been appearing in the garden for some time. I had been puzzled when a sponge disappeared from the top of the garden shed and re-appeared on the ground, but the mystery was solved one afternoon. Little Fox was lying on the grass, lovingly chewing something he was holding between his paws. An hour later he was still there. When he'd eventually gone back under the fence I went down into the garden to see what had kept him so engrossed. On the grass lay a woollen mouse without its tail, presumably stolen from a domestic pet. A week or so later, an orange appeared and moved around the garden. As our relationship evolved, I was able to join in with the fox's play, throwing the sponge for him to fetch. Instead of bringing it to me like a dog, he would retrieve it from where it had fallen and take it a safe distance away.

But there were limits to how close I wanted the relationship to get. With the summer in full swing, Little Fox was showing a definite interest in my living quarters. One afternoon while I was sitting on the sun lounger, he started up the back steps, making decisively for the open door. I was not keen on him going into the flat, fearing that my shoes would go for toys. 'Come down,' I said firmly. 'Now'. He stopped and looked at me. Then, looking back at the kitchen door, he mounted another step. 'No,' I said, even more firmly. 'Come back down.' I pointed to the garden behind him. 'There.' Reluctantly, he turned round and obeyed.

If all this sounds like the kind of domestic relationship you would have with a pet, it did indeed have that quality of ease and normality. But it's important to add that Little Fox could also be timid, even skittish, and would at times run and dive back under the fence when he saw me. He was still a wild animal and, as I had grown up with pets, neither aspect of his behaviour surprised me.

But there was one thing that did: the expression in his eyes. Science tends to fight shy of any suggestion that animals have expressions readable by humans because, it argues, they do not share our emotions. It's a viewpoint that leaves only the observation of behaviour as a way of interpreting what is going on inside animal minds. But over the course of that spring and summer, I repeatedly saw feelings I recognised in Little Fox's eyes. They ranged from anxiety and wariness to contentment and friendliness, with the most pronounced expression being a kind of intelligent interest.

Most people, not being subject to the constraints of scientific research, read emotions on the faces of animals all the time. Cats and dogs, the last of the animals to live with and alongside us, are a constant reminder that other living beings have feelings and needs. For us, a visual species, the look of an animal is key to assessing the mood of those we meet in public spaces: the contented blink of a cat as it sits on a window sill, the craving for acknowledgement of a friendly dog. And so the question arises: if the characteristic look of a cat is satisfaction, and that of a dog hopefulness, what is the look of a fox? I would say it is curiosity.

∾

July. I am soon to go away for almost six weeks and will no longer be able to feed my fox. But I have a plan: I'll buy a big bag of dog biscuits and ask my downstairs neighbour to throw some over the fence between our two gardens each day. My long-suffering neighbour agrees, but the difficulty is that the fence is the opposite end of the garden from where I normally leave food. And so a period of training ensues. When Little Fox appears expectantly, I point to the new feeding ground where I've left some biscuits. Getting them involves passing me on the sun lounger and approaching the building inhabited by humans: not things he's keen on, unless on his terms. But I keep pointing to the biscuits by the fence until, with some reluctance, he runs past me to get to them.

One afternoon he is comfortable enough to approach as soon as I've put the biscuits down. But his demeanour clearly signals that he won't eat while I'm nearby, so I retreat around the corner and resume my pruning. A moment or two later, he's standing at the corner, looking at me with ears cocked. There is something about their angle which says, as clearly as ears can: 'You still here? I told you I didn't want you near while I'm eating.' I laugh, put down the secateurs, and go inside.

The feeding plan works. In the early autumn I return to find evidence of continued vulpine life in the garden. A pot of vanilla yoghurt is lying, licked clean, by the feeding site. The washing line above dangles in two, the section with the clothes pegs neatly nipped out and lying on the ground. I have missed Little Fox and can't wait to see him in the fur. I get the remains of the biscuits from my neighbour and continue to put out food.

But, as the days turned into weeks, Little Fox fails to appear. The mouse I've brought back for him lies on the ground ignored, its tail firmly on. As the autumn evenings draw in, I come to accept that he's gone, that it's the end of my fox friendship.

Except that it isn't, quite. One summer evening a year later I am coming down the same road where I met Pampas Grass Cub when I am brought up short. There, on the corner which turns into my street, is a fox standing staring at me. He has the same slight build as Little Fox, the same dullish colouring, but is clearly an adult. For a minute or two I stand rooted to the spot, talking softly, something about remembering. He stands uncertainly and stares. Then, very slowly, he turns around and goes on his way.

After that, in the lighter months, I often see him on his rounds from my front window. His street patrol starts in the early evening with a check of the bins outside the houses opposite and involves a mix of weaving through front gardens and trotting briskly down the pavement. 'He looks busy, but efficient,' says a friend as we watch from the bay window. And then I see him no more. I assume he's gone the way of most urban foxes, dying within two or three years. In my mind, I let him go. But Little Fox has grown up against the odds, sought human help and successfully re-wilded himself. It is hard to think of it as anything but a story with a happy ending.

The relationship between foxes and humans in modern Britain is a relatively recent one, born of a complex set of circumstances that encompasses the country's lack of dangerous animals and the quintessentially British attachment to land. The Vermin Acts passed by Henry VIII placed communities under an obligation to kill all creatures considered a threat to crops and livestock; with the dying out of wolves and bears, the fox became the countryside's only serious predator. It was a mammal worthy of hunting, a sport which, by the eighteenth century, had evolved into a national pastime that gave form to the landowning classes' sense of what it meant to be British. Fox hunting had become a powerful symbol of country life. In the twentieth century, as cities sprawled into the countryside, suburban dwellers began to notice the presence of foxes in their streets and gardens: an ideal habitat for such adaptable mammals. As the urban fox population grew, so did human concerns: foxes were seen as pests which despoiled gardens and spread the pavements with rubbish. For a few decades, the London authorities attempted to cull the fox population, before accepting that this did not work – an empty territory simply attracted other foxes – and advocating that concerned householders use deterrence methods instead. But while officialdom accepted that humans and foxes could co-exist, public hostility to foxes grew. By the 1990s, media reports about them attacking pets and children both reflected and fuelled a belief that the fox was dangerous, the one British animal who predated on humans, even in their own homes. [2]

English children's literature provides two vividly opposing portraits of the fox: the cunning predator who persuades Jemima Puddle-Duck to bring her own stuffing, and the enterprising, resourceful father who outwits the evil farmers that seek to destroy him. In Beatrix Potter, the fox is humanised into a gentleman-conman with 'sandy coloured whiskers' and a 'bushy tail' who reads the newspaper; Roald Dahl paints him as a Robin Hood-style figure who not only does what is necessary to feed his family, but saves a whole community of underground animals from starvation. But whether villain or hero, the fox is defined in terms of the role it plays in human society. In the 21st century, following the 2005 ban on hunting, these opposing attitudes have formed sides worthy of a civil war, with one seeking to continue the tradition and hunt saboteurs and wildlife campaigners on the other.

I encountered some of these extreme attitudes during my time with Little Fox. Some friends and neighbours saw my accidental fox-fostering as I did, a rare opportunity to experience a relationship with a wild creature that was as natural as it was special. But others reacted against my animal friendship with vehemence: it was wrong to encourage foxes; did I know that, given the chance, they attacked babies? The curious thing was that I couldn't predict who would take which view, and was surprised when certain friends cited a tabloid story about a fox attacking a sleeping baby as categorical evidence of vulpine evil.

I suspected that modern British foxes were carrying a heavy freight of ambivalence about our relationship with wild creatures more generally, something that had to do with the loss of an ancient kinship that went back to humans' first experiences on earth. 'In the beginning, Adam and the animals were together in Eden,' the psychologist James Hillman puts it poetically, evoking a lost utopia 'at the beginning of the story of the world' in which there was a mutual seeing between the animal and the human. [3] In his seminal essay *Why Look At Animals?* John Berger elaborates on the significance of this kinship: as man's first companions, animals acted as the mediating link between nature and culture, thereby helping to breach the state of isolation that is part of the human condition. Animals' distinctness from man was essential to this relationship: from their separate existence across a gulf unbreachable by a common language, they brought something that humans lacked and could not obtain in any other way: 'With their parallel lives, animals offer man a companionship which is different from any offered by human exchange.' [4]

Millennia later, at what Hillman says may turn out to be 'the ending of the story of the world', animals are vanishing, in some cases quite literally, from the earth, their habitats rendered lifeless. [5] Meanwhile, their images are everywhere: on our TV screens, on the internet and adorning our stationary, our clothes, our homes. Berger pinpoints the beginning of the peculiarly modern way of seeing animals to the first zoos, established as animals began to disappear from daily life under the process of industrialisation. In zoos, animals become spectacle: denaturalised, flat representations whose purpose is to satisfy the human gaze that are, at bottom, an illustration of how their living counterparts have been pushed to the margins of human experience.

Yet despite the gloomy truth of these analyses, if you look closely you can also see signs of a deep yearning for kinship with wild creatures in our everyday lives. Obvious examples can be found in the British love of nature, in the national habit of feeding the birds, and the delight with which people report encounters with animals as privileged moments which take them, briefly, out of the human world. Vast reserves of time, money and energy are poured into conservation projects which, as well as representing an attempt to compensate for the damage done by humans to animals, testify to our fear of being left to live in the world alone. In this sphere of activity, animals are neither conscripted for the companionship they give as our pets nor reared to put meat on our plates, but enabled to live in their own way.

English literature has a little-known tale of one man's journey to acceptance of the wildness of the wild. In *Lady into Fox*, a happily married Victorian gentleman called Mr Tebrick is out for a walk with his wife when he finds that she has turned into a fox. [6] Ever the loving husband, he dismisses the servants and tries to continue a normal married life, draping the vixen in a dressing jacket of flowered silk and hand feeding her pieces of bread and butter. But as his wife's behaviour becomes more and more fox-like, Tebrick realises that she needs her freedom and releases her into the woods. After a period of separation, their relationship is re-established on new terms, with the vixen proudly showing him her cubs and making him part of the family. In his new role as uncle to a litter of foxes, he discovers a kind of animal-happiness previously unknown to him: 'What if they were foxes? Mr Tebrick found that he could be happy with them. As the weather was hot, he lay out there all night, first playing hide and seek with them in the dark till, missing his vixen and the cubs proving obstreperous, he lay down and was soon asleep.' When he awoke, 'all human customs and institutions seemed to him nothing but folly; for said he, "I would exchange all my life as a man for my happiness now, and even now I retain almost all of the ridiculous conceptions of a man. The beasts are happier and I will deserve that happiness as best I can."' [7]

With this uplifting moral lesson under her belt, the reader is not heartbroken when the story ends, somewhat predictably, with the vixen dying in her husband's arms after having been fatally wounded by a pack of hounds.

My own experience of developing a bond with a wild creature and then having to let go had given me a new sense of what might be possible in human-animal relations. But I was well aware of the limitations of my experience: my summer with Little Fox was a one-off, and unsupported by any established practice. I decided that at some point, when time and lifestyle allowed, I would volunteer in a wildlife centre and see what humans could do for foxes when they made a collective effort.

The opportunity came five years later after I had moved to the South West. On a day-course at the wildlife rescue centre Secret World, I learnt that anyone taking a wild creature into captivity has a legal obligation to care for it. [8] An animal cannot be released back into wild if its ability to survive is compromised which means that in some cases an animal has to be 'euthanised'. The organisation's founder, Pauline Kidner, also introduced us to the softer side of animal care with the story of the frightened deer who stopped struggling once she had seen rescuers release the other deer they were cutting free from the fence they were trapped in. 'Wildlife knows when you are trying to help it,' she said.

At lunchtime, I stopped outside the enclosure containing the resident foxes. Their former lives among people had made it impossible to release the three vixens back into the wild; they were now too tame to flee the humans who might kill them. So they were living, comfortably ever after, in a large outside enclosure on view to the public. Not that you could necessarily see them: the pen was filled with long grass and patches of nettles, as well as various pieces of wood and plastic in which to hide. But on this fine autumn day, one of the vixens was stretched out on a wooden platform beneath the tree. I stood and watched her for a while; it was strange to see a fox looking this relaxed, blinking in repose as she took in the midday sun.

At the end of the day, I approached Pauline and explained that I was a writer with an interest in foxes: was there anywhere in the South West I could work with them? I imagined she might know of somewhere in Bristol, the fox-capital of the region. Her response surprised me. 'You can come here,' she said immediately.

An exchange of emails followed. Pauline suggested that I start in the spring when the fox cubs arrived and follow their progress until they were released as adults in the autumn. 'It would be best to start coming once the fox cubs arrive and then see it through to their final release,' she wrote. 'Your day would be as a volunteer and whilst we can let you see what happens with the fox cubs, there will be other jobs too! I'm sure with plenty of notice we can make sure that the process of rehab falls into your day. I have also copied Tristan in on this email as he is our release manager and he may be able to include you when he is surveying a release site or taking a group of foxes for release.'

The commitment would involve a long drive, further than

I'd anticipated going, and the kind of physical work well out of my comfort zone. But the experience promised to give me a real insight into the development of foxes and what happens when people got together in a deliberate, organised attempt to help wildlife.

DON'T TALK TO THE ANIMALS

The following March I drive over to Secret World for my induction as a volunteer. After a talk about manual handling and what to do in the event of a fire, the small group is given a tour of the site.

Twenty-five years after wild animals were first cared for in Pauline's farmhouse, the facilities are a motley collection of buildings. Brick outbuildings serve as the reception, store and treatment rooms, while the smartly-renovated Bluebell Barn, named after a badger dear to Pauline's heart, hosts meetings and training sessions. The organisation is at the beginning of a phase of fundraising and construction which, it is hoped, will eventually result in facilities fit for 21st century wildlife rescue. Some of the original buildings have been demolished and, in the interim, much of the animal care is being done in portacabins. Millie Block, a long low building purpose-built in the early 2000s to house the mammals and some of the larger birds, looks old for its age.

Inside, the concrete corridor is chilly and the rows of doors to the animal pens give it the feel of of a prison block. We walk along and glance through the windows. Some, being small and tiled for ease of cleaning, are positively cell-like, but others are large with access to outside runs. We take turns to peep through one spy hole and see a young badger snuffling about in the warmth of a heat lamp. The group talks in whispers: we've been told it's important that animals destined for release back into the wild don't get used to the sound of human voices. Then we go into a barn to do a practical task: cleaning out the hedgehogs. These, the trainer tells me, are one group of animals that it's fine to address, as experience suggests they are unaffected by human speech. He holds up a towel and I see a hedgehog for the first time since childhood, a face of story-book sweetness poking out of its prickles. A black webbed foot stretches out and then recoils; the hog is not much interested in anything but sleep.

On the drive home I think about the impulse to talk to animals. The human yearning to communicate with our fellow creatures is age-old: Berger, in writing of the 'unspeaking companionship' that animals gave early people, notes legends about 'exceptional beings' such as Orpheus possessed of the enviable ability to talk to them. [9] Eighteenth-century writing is full of references to 'dumb animals', testimony of the sadness at our inability to talk to the creatures who lived alongside us. The magic of some of the greatest cultural influences on my childhood – *The Lion, the Witch and the Wardrobe* and the 1967 film *Doctor Doolittle* – derives largely from the beautifully-realised fantasy that, at last, humans and animals can communicate. For me, a verbal creature whose love of foxes began because she felt impelled to speak to a rustling bush, the injunction to keep silent goes against my natural inclination. But I understand the reason for the rule, and will do my best to keep it.

It is another month before I am allocated my first shift. Looking at the staff noticeboard on site, I note with surprise that it's to be spent in the Hospital Rooms, a set of porta-cabins lined with cages of orphaned nestlings.

I am trained by long-standing volunteer Rhi. She's a good teacher, showing me how to hold a wooden stick loaded with food – a mixture of cat food and crushed insects – almost vertically above the bird and, when it opens its beak, to pop the food in. Tickling the side of mouth encourages a reluctant bird to gape, but most birds are eager to feed and I find that many will eat more than the recommended six portions.

As I move from cage to cage, I'm struck by the differences between groups. Some birds queue as they wait for their turn at the stick; others compete chaotically, jumping at it from various directions. A few, having taken one or two portions, treat it as a threat, hopping away to the back of the cage in fear.

A recently-hatched robin in the corner incubator, bald except for a bit of fluff on the top of his head, won't open his beak. He had been brought in that morning, having been attacked by a cat. The general view is that he won't survive. But attempts are made, every half an hour, to get him to take a drop of the creamy neonate offered in a pipette.

'Can you do a hot glove?'

It takes me a moment to realise the question is addressed to me. Although I've been there for a couple of hours, the staff member in charge hasn't acknowledged my presence; it's almost as if she hasn't seen me. An extra pair of hands is needed to help another food refusenik, a young blackbird with an injured wing whose quills are only just starting to emerge from the bare skin. A cold bird will not feed and the hot glove – a latex glove filled with hot water – acts as a kind of hot water bottle. I fill and hand over a glove and find that, suddenly, I have entered the circle of animal carers.

By the end of the morning, Rhi and I have worked our way around the room. Every cage has been cleaned, disinfected and lined with fresh towels and periodically I've gone outside to cut greenery on which the birds can perch. Each bird has been weighed, with members of groups distinguished from each other by a dab of Tippex which names them 'One Mark', 'Two Mark' or 'No Mark'. Feeds punctuate the cleaning and weighing; the babies are fed at hourly intervals; the older birds every four hours. Amid all this activity I find that my sense of wonder at being so close to birds I usually see only from a distance is lost behind the work of the avian nurse. And yet the act of feeding a bird is so absorbing that the rest of the world seems to disappear. When fixed on the eager beak in front of me, I notice that I too find it difficult to acknowledge the people around me.

But where are the foxes? Apart from one of the resident foxes – sunbathing again – I have yet to see one. So at lunchtime, I pop into Millie Block to take a first look at the cubs I am supposed to be following. 'No, sorry,' I'm told curtly by the staffer on duty. 'We're trying to keep human contact to a minimum.' I try to explain my agreement with Pauline; he says he will talk to her about 'what she meant'.

The following week I am back with the birds. I find a manager, have another word, and am transferred to Millie Block. Someone waves a laminated card stipulating that only staff members can handle foxes in front of me. Then I watch from the door while the staffer shuts three cubs into a plastic carrier so I can clean their pen. The cubs are about eight weeks old, with brown-fur faces that resemble teddy bears. Although it's not customary to give names to foxes destined for release, one cub has so impressed the staff with his personality that they have dubbed him Seamus. Adventurous and unafraid, he craves the attention of his human carers. 'They will start crying,' the staffer warns as she departs. 'They want you to take notice, but you have to ignore them.'

With the door closed, the concentrated smell of urine and

faeces catches my throat, almost making me gag. As I scoop up the poo, crying comes from inside the carrier. It is a piteous sound that hovers between the scream of a seagull and the wordless anguish of a human baby with something of the otherworldly about it. I feel myself smiling grimly as I get on with the clean, moping the floor with Anistel and putting down fresh blankets. Then I fetch their food - a bowl of dog meat for each cub and some chicks to scatter around. Once the staff member has opened the carrier, I watch through the peephole. Seamus is the first fox out. He wanders casually towards a bowl of food but, as soon as he sees a chick, abruptly changes course and scoops the fluffy corpse into his jaw. The two other cubs emerge soon afterwards and explore their freshly-cleaned environment. One gazes up the tiled wall, as if looking for an exit. Then he sniffs his way round the rest of the cell as if it's a different place. The others are preoccupied by the new blanket, tugging at it and rolling around in its folds.

It takes another week and another word with management to make my transfer to Millie Block permanent. In the meantime, someone gives me the low-down on the organisation: now at retirement age, the founder has stepped back and the new chief executive, the second in a couple of years, is focused on making corporate-style changes. There is a general lack of communication, and if if you're not part of the management-elite that makes up the inner circle, you won't know what's going on. The strict division of tasks between staff and volunteers was introduced fairly recently and was, in her view, more about instituting a hierarchy among humans than animal care.

I sigh. I'd been hoping, by working with animals, to get away from this kind of all-too-human politics, but what I was experiencing was definitely more *Animal Farm* than *Doctor Doolittle*. 'Yes, it's here too,' agrees my source.

Still, at last I am on Millie Block where the foxes are. The day begins with the cleaning of every pen and ends with sluicing out of the long corridor. The morning and afternoon feeds must be prepared according to the specific requirements of each animal: big-eating badgers get a large tray bearing dog meat, sausages, scrambled egg and, to ween them off their mother's milk, something sweet such as a jam sandwich or a few custard creams. The otters in the pond outside are taken a bucket of whole fish. In between comes the washing and sterilising of dozens of bowls and the never-ending fetching of supplies from the various buildings around the site.

At the laundry portacabin, the labour is positively heroic. Industrial washing machines are in constant churn, the volunteer-laundress moving continuously between the wheelbarrows full of dirty linen and the washing lines on the grass outside. As I deliver the latest batch of filthy blankets, I stop to chat with Pat. She doesn't even stop for lunch, she tells me, grabbing mouthfuls in between folding clean towels. She has dealt with the biological waste of three children, while I have largely escaped dealing with excrement. Despite our different backgrounds we agree that we wouldn't clean up all this poo for humans.

But while I am regularly cleaning up fox poo, I am barely seeing any actual foxes. For the most part, they shoot into the wooden box provided for sleep and sanctuary as soon as they hear the door opening. But one day, as I follow the staffer into a pen, we find a tiny cub sitting composedly behind a straw bale. He blinks at me: it feels like a smile.

The staffer shoos him into the box with the others, lowers the wooden slats, and I get on with the clean. No sound comes from this group of cubs – four orphans from different litters – as I gather the soiled blankets and newspaper and mop the tiled surfaces. It's a stark contrast to the behaviour of Seamus, whose screams are often heard ringing down the corridor.

At lunchtime I pay a visit to the hospital rooms. 'So you do miss the birds,' smiles Rhi, who is newly in love with a crow. She had at first been nervous about feeding him, having never dealt with a corvid before. I understand her trepidation: with their size, pronounced beaks and apparent confidence, corvids can seem threatening to humans. But in the event, she was charmed by his attempts to cuddle up to her as she feeds him. 'He likes being stroked under the chin, and he purrs at me. Have a stroke.' The crow, mouth gaping bright red, lifts his beak and offers his chin. The feathers underneath are soft. From now on, I'll be regarding crows with a more tender eye too.

Back on Millie Block, part of the afternoon is spent cleaning out a vacated badger pen - a huge, exhausting task that involves shovelling out all the soiled woodchip and taking the bags of contaminated waste to the dumpsters.

At home in the bath I reflect on the redeeming moments of a tough day: the welcoming blink of a fox cub and the soft-feathered chin of a young crow.

'Alex, the FOX MAMA is here!'

Rhi has sent another volunteer to fetch me, and the two of us hasten to the staff portacabin. My fellow volunteers know that I'm not getting enough access to foxes for my research and hope to help. They introduce me to the Fox Mama, a large, tattooed woman who has arrived for her weekly visit with the resident foxes. Because Julie's been coming for two years and, unlike the time-pressed staffers, spends time playing with the foxes, she has a strong bond with them. If I accompany her into their pen, some of her status as a human worth knowing will rub off on me.

And so it is that as soon as we enter the pen with washing up bowls full of dog meat and chicks, all three foxes come out of the long grass and approach us with interest.

Mia, a vixen whose wide face is framed with thick white fur, is the boldest. Megan and April are not far behind, and the expression in their eyes is friendly. With Julie's encouragement, I hand feed the foxes their chicks, noticing how gently they take the limp yellow body from my hand. Even the brush of teeth against my fingers doesn't bother me; it's like feeding a trusted dog. After that, we distribute some biscuit treats but find that, after a few mouthfuls, the foxes stop eating and take them away to cache in the grass.

Then it is play time. I stand back to take pictures as Julie sits down on the grass and allows the foxes to run at her, jumping on her lap, licking her face and hair. At one point, the mouth of one of the vixens meets hers in what looks for all the world like a kiss. My digital shutter clicks too late.

'That was a good grooming,' says Julie. Sometimes, she says, the smell of the foxes lingers on her after she's played with them, and she is given a wide berth in the supermarket queue. I am welcome to come and visit them with her every time she comes, she adds. 'But they'll probably wee on you.'

In the event, personal circumstances stop her from coming again, so I don't get a repeat visit with the Fox Mama. But the resident foxes never forget how well-connected I am. Ever after, I only have to stand by the fence of their pen and Mia will emerge out of the long grass and trot towards me. Then she sits by the fence and waits, blinking and licking her lips. If I can't lay my hands on any dog biscuits, I steal a custard cream from the badger supplies and crumble it up as the other two vixens appear.

I am, meanwhile, getting used to the characteristic smell

of Millie Block: urine and faeces, straw and woodchip, all mixed up with disinfectant and the odours of particular species which give it an earthy pungency so distinctive that I can easily recall it at home. When I am there, I'm increasingly noticing the different ways that people respond to stress. The workload is unvaryingly huge, while the numbers of personnel change day by day, depending on how many volunteers there are. One staff member is so stressed she can barely communicate, while another sails through the same conditions with a zen-like calm. The teenager on work experience I meet in the kitchen seems bemused, and I ask him how far his first experience of animal care matches his expectations. He pauses a moment and then says: 'There's a lot more poo than I expected.'

THREE LITTLE FOXES

May. One weekend I go to Paris to visit an old friend and her children and find myself in the middle of a dispute about how foxes should be coloured in. No problem: I flip open my laptop to reveal pictures of the resident foxes at Secret World and instantly resolve the matter: legs should be coloured in brown. Drawing completed, each child writes a story on the back. Six-year-old Louis' tale of a hunting fox ends with a successful killing and a chicken dinner, while his elder sister's concludes with a philosophical note that neatly sums up conflicting attitudes to the animal: 'The fox: friend or enemy to humanity?'

Back in Somerset, apart from the occasional glimpse of a tail disappearing into a box, I barely see a fox, never mind following the progress of a group. I am thinking of cutting my loses on The Fox Project when my fortunes abruptly change. Millie Block staffer Sarah has taken up my cause and suggests that I follow the three orphaned cubs who arrived from Devon over the weekend. After approaching management again, I am granted permission to observe the group regularly. The cubs' story exemplifies the plight of rural foxes: their mother had been shot by a farmer while they were still nursing; they would have died had they not been rescued by another farmer who had taken them to the safety of an outbuilding and called a contact in the rescue world, Jess had called Secret World, and the system had kicked in. A response driver had been dispatched to collect them and they had been driven to the rescue centre.

I take the clipboard with the orphaned cubs' notes from the door of their pen. There is one male, one female and one sex unknown; they weigh between 1.15 and 1.50 kilograms - a bag of flour, at most. Then I take a first look at them through the peephole. All three are sitting on top of the wooden box. They are small and brown, a bit beyond the kitten-like stage of vulpine infancy but not quite into foxhood. One is curled up in the corner, but the other two seem to know they are being looked at and stare at the door, rigid with fear. One is shaking, his abdomen pumping rapidly. I withdraw and go back to the kitchen.

'Will you help me shut them in?' Sarah hasn't been able to get the cubs into their box for cleaning because they keep trying to bite her. She thinks they haven't even been in their box yet, possibly associating it with entrapment. We don latex gloves and she hands me a piece of board and a towel for protection. Rather than picking them up and putting them into the box, we will try corralling the foxes until they run into its dark sanctuary themselves.

We look through the window of the pen. The cubs are still huddled together on top of the box, the smallest in the corner. On seeing us, the other two barely react but the middle one yawns. We steel ourselves and Sarah opens the door. Immediately, the foxes jump off the box and squeeze themselves into the corner between the box and the tiled wall. There isn't enough space to accommodate all three, so they sit on top of each other. A strange noise between coughing and growling comes from the pile.

I block their exit while Sarah tries to encourage them towards the box with a towel. The foxes stay where they are, cowering and spluttering. 'If only they could understand,' she says in frustration. There is no alternative: she picks them up by the scruff, one by one, and puts them into the box. We drop the wooden slats into place, sealing both its exits. Silence falls and I get on with the clean. When the floor and walls have been disinfected and dried, I fetch some straw and put down three bowls of dog food, each topped with a chick. Finally, I choose three squeaker toys of different colours and sizes and scatter them around the pen.

With the slats of the box lifted, I watch them through the peephole. Two of the foxes come out almost immediately and investigate their changed environment, sniffing at the straw, jumping on and off the box and examining the corners of the pen as if looking for a way out. Then, noticing the food, the boldest goes to one of the bowls, picks up a chick and takes it to the corner. Meanwhile, the third fox emerges cautiously. Seeing him, Bold Fox runs to the second bowl and flips the chick into his jaw. Then he picks up the smallest toy - a red squeaker - and disappears with his haul into the box.

I continue to watch them for a good ten minutes. This time, they are oblivious to my presence as they play and explore, running in and out of the box, chasing each other and rolling around. After seeing them frozen in fear, it is a delight to see.

∼

Late May. The cubs are to be moved to a bigger pen with a

window to mimic conditions in the wild when they would now be emerging from the den and starting to explore the outside world. Around them, Millie Block is dark and quiet. In an attempt to make life in tune with the animals' natural nocturnal rhythms, morning feeds have been significantly reduced and the bulk of the food put out in the evening.

I continue to watch how the foxes respond to their food. A pattern of behaviour has been established: Bold Fox comes out of the box first and grabs a chick, followed quickly by a second. Middle Cub takes the third chick, and Small Cub gets nothing. On one occasion I observe him going to the bowl to find it chickless, taking a mouthful of dog food and wandering off. I fetch another chick from the kitchen for him, but when I open the door, all the foxes skedaddle into the box. The next mealtime, Bold Fox takes all three chicks.

'There's always a dominant one,' shrugs a staffer at coffee. But Sarah says we can't have the cubs losing weight, and the notes confirm that others have noticed how one fox gets all the chicks. I am wondering whether the distribution of food should be left to nature, but then I read that when the runt of a litter isn't getting much food, it pesters the mother. Since the foxes are in human care, we are in loco parentis. Sarah agrees that we need to try to bring about a more equal distribution of chicks.

I walk down the corridor, chicks in hand. The plan, while Bold Fox is busy collecting the chicks from the bowls, is to put the extra ones in the way of the other two cubs. But when I open the door, the clunk of the bolt echoes down the corridor and the cubs scram into the box. I put the door to and fetch more chicks. My new plan is to push the door open quietly and throw the chicks to the cubs at the far end of the pen while Bold Fox hoovers up the ones on the floor. But every time I open the door, he peeps out from behind the box. He is watching my every move and is perfectly positioned to run out and gather up any new chicks, along with those already on the floor. I duck to the side, hoping he'll think I've gone. But when I next look in, I see the tips of his ears above the box. We're in a stand-off, he and I. After a few more minutes, I give up. The fox has won.

Sarah says that scattering the chicks may not work when the dominant fox can go round and collect them; she has another idea. When she goes into the pen to replenish the straw in the box, I follow her, chicks in hand. She lifts the lid. The three foxes are curled up slightly apart; they look up at us warily. I had been confident I could distinguish Bold Fox and Small Fox by their size and allocate chicks to the deserving. But now they are in the box, I can't tell them apart. I half-throw, half-place a chick in front of each one. The foxes look bemused. The chicks stay where they fell. Sarah closes the box and we leave the pen.

Sounds of growly slurping come from inside the box. I've no idea which of the foxes is eating the chicks; we've reached the limit of what we can do.

Laundry pile-up. Pat's on holiday and hasn't been replaced. The piles of towels and bedding are growing outside the laundry; Everyone is supposed to be pitching in with the washing, but No One is taking responsibility. In Millie Block we have run out of clean essentials. I dive into a pile fresh out of a washing machine to get some mop heads and feel impelled to hang out the rest of the wash. It's a bottomless pit: several machine-loads of sheets have been compressed into the wheelbarrow so that the more washing you hang out, the more you find. Digging deeper, it turns out that someone has put wet washing on top of dry ... I could spend half the morning sorting this one wheelbarrow out, so I grab what I need and go back to my post. At lunchtime those of us in the staff kitchen hear a gagging sound coming from the laundry area. The maintenance man has been charged with clearing the piles of soiled fabrics, but he's a sensitive chap and the task turns his stomach. Everyone finds this incredibly funny.

On Millie Block, it is a day for weighing foxes. I help to carry Seamus' group in wire baskets across the site to the assessment room and notice how their brown fur is giving way to red. As Sarah lifts one fox out of the basket, he slips from her grasp and runs into the corner of the portacabin. She dives into the corner, gets him by the scruff and places him on the metal scale. He stands quivering while someone else records the weight on the notes. The weighing of the others is accomplished without incident and we carry the foxes back to Millie Block. Seamus is exempt because, as Sarah puts it, 'he is fat'.

Then it's the turn of the three little foxes. A new staff member is being trained in handling, so there are three of us in the pen. The foxes cower in the box, spluttering. Sarah lifts the lift, scruffs one and lowers him into the cage. The trainee catches the second but is too nervous to tangle with Bold Fox, so Sarah scruffs him too. Then we each carry a caged fox across to the hospital room. Mine stays standing, his paws constantly shifting to keep his balance: is he preparing for possible escape? This time, the weighing is accomplished without difficulty and, to our surprise, the difference between the foxes is not great: 2.65 kg, 2.40 and 2.45. So, Sarah concludes, two of them are making up for the lack of chicks with meat.

Later, I am sent to feed Seamus' group, now occupying a large pen with an outside run. When I open the door, Seamus is prowling around as if waiting for me; the other foxes have hidden themselves. I try to disperse the chicks in such a way that the others will have a chance to grab them when they come out of the box, but Seamus stalks me around the pen. I try to usher him outside, but he simply mirrors my movements and we end up doing a little dance.

FIRST FREEDOM

A scorching day in June. It's not my day to volunteer, but I am making a special trip to Secret World to observe the moving of the three foxes to an outside pen by Tristan, the release manager. The idea is that from now on, the foxes will have minimum contact with humans. Come the autumn, when they are fully grown and have learnt how to live outside, they will be taken to a site of a friendly landowner and set free. But before they are moved to their pre-release pen, the cubs need a medical check and vaccinations.

It is time for the afternoon feeds. While we wait for the vet, I am dispatched into various pens with bowls of food and water. It seems that the heat is putting the animals off their food; one fox I serve approaches a dish, sniffs the chick on top of the dog meat and retires without taking it.

The vet's visit is accomplished in a flash. Bold Fox splutters at us and one of the others wees on Tristan. But within a few minutes, all three have been vaccinated and secured in a large wire cage. Tristan covers it with a sheet; the foxes will be calmer if they can't see us or be seen. Then we each take a handle and make our way to the pens at the edge of the site.

The foxes' new home looks inviting. It is big and green, with long, lush grass and clumps of nettles the cubs can disappear into. There's a wooden box to sleep in, and a board leaning against the fence for further cover. Until the day they are caught and taken to their release site, the foxes can avoid all human contact if they choose. And yet they are not free: the high wire fence extends all the way round, covering even the top of the pen.

Having deposited the cage in the centre of the pen, I step back: the release will provide a rare chance to take some pictures of the foxes. "How will they react?' I ask Tristan as I ready my camera. 'I don't know,' he replies. 'Some shoot straight out of the cage, while others are reluctant to leave.' It's been known, he adds, for some foxes to go a bit mad when they're first let out, spinning themselves round in compulsive circles. So, rather than tipping them out of the cage as some people do, his approach will be to raise the slat and allow them to leave in their own time.

'Ready?' His hand is on the slat.

The next instant, a cub shoots out of the cage, bounds away and disappears into grass at the end of the pen. A second fox follows almost immediately.

But the third, the smallest, stays in the cage, his head turning hesitantly as he tries to take in this wide new world. He puts his head out and, for a moment, it seems as if he too is about to leave. But then he pulls it back in and continues to stand uncertainly in the cage. After a few more moments, Tristan taps the wire with a stick to encourage him to leave, but to no effect. Small Fox seems less bothered by the presence of humans than the prospect of exposure in this strange green place. He continues to study it from inside the cage, opening and shutting his jaw in a gesture I've become familiar with. [10]

Head out; head in. My camera clicks. The indecision makes for good fox-watching. Then, with a leap, the third fox is out and all three are out of sight, somewhere at the back of the pen.

I stand and watch for a few minutes. Most of the time all I can see is grass, although now and then a pair of ears becomes visible. Two of the foxes are coursing the edge of the pen, following the fence in way that suggests both exploration and play. First they run behind each other, then they turn and run towards each other. Pounce! One jumps, as if diving on prey. I realise that I'm witnessing the first free movements of their lives. Eventually Tristan manages to prise me out of the pen so that he can get on with his work.

The next morning, I am back for my regular shift. It's barely nine, but the heat is rising. Sheets are being draped over the outside pens to give the animals some shade and fans placed in the hospital wing to cool the panting birds.

When I arrive in Millie Block, Sarah suggests that I go straight up to the pre-release pens. I'm not sure I'll see anything except perhaps some ears, I say ... 'Go on,' she says. 'You'll still get an idea of how your three are doing by seeing where they are.'

She's right. In the wire mesh corridor between the two rows of pens I find a fellow-volunteer with a barrow full of food. I can just about manage to carry the bowls over to the pen, but when I get to the heavy wire door, I need to put them down in the grass to draw back the bolt. And so it is that, squatting down by the fence, I see the form of a fox stretched out in the long grass. He must be flaked out in the heat like the rest of us. Peering through the fence, I see the blue-green shimmer of bluebottles crawling on him. It's strange that he's making no effort to flick them off.

'O no oh no oh no ...' It's an involuntary wail, and it's coming from me. For a moment, my upper body is choked with sobs. Then I pull myself together. The other volunteer comes over and peers over my shoulder. This is definitely a dead body; the jaw hangs open, the fur is rumpled. At the joint of a front leg, the flat surface of a bone is sticking out, completely clean of any flesh or blood.

Grimly, we wade through the long grass of the pen to check on the other two foxes. We find one curled up in the box, the other crouching between the board and the fence. There's a moment of relief and then I go back to the main buildings to tell the head of animal care. Laura evinces no surprise. 'It happens,' she says matter-of-factly.

She comes back to the pen with me to collect the body, squatting down to conduct an informal post-mortem on the path. The bare-boned joint is not broken and the body is limp, suggesting that it's already passed the rigour mortis stage. The open eyes are rheumy and bloodshot; it looks as though he's been dead since last night. Foxes often jump and climb, so this one may have got his leg caught in something and then bled to death.

Laura picks the dead fox up by his feet and, as the limp corpse dangles from her hand, I run a finger down his forehead fur. It is as soft as that of a high-quality cuddly toy: I've been longing to touch a fox ever since my garden days with Little Fox, but there has never been a moment when it's seemed right to do so. The other volunteer and I follow behind as she carries the body back to the main buildings; my intention is to coolly document the process of what happens next. But in truth I feel more like a chief mourner at a funeral, a feeling enhanced by the big black hat and scarf I'm wearing to keep off the sun. As the little procession makes its way across the campus we are met by gloomy glances and the phrase 'it happens'.

In the assessment room, neither the first nor the second scanner show a reading; the fox's chip may be faulty. Weighing may tell us which of the three it is and there's no need to fetch the notes: I have the weights of all three from the previous week in my head. Laura puts the body on the scales. 2.5 kilograms – it looks as if it's Middle Fox.

We take him to the outbuilding which doubles up as mortuary and food store. It's always struck me as a strange place, with chest freezers full of animal corpses lining the walls and dustbins full of dried food filling the floor. But this juxtaposition of life and death has a logic, for the bodies of dead animals in one freezer are kept to be fed to the living, so becoming part of the cycle of life. Middle Fox is not for consumption: Laura puts the body into a yellow bag marked 'For Incineration' and deposits the bag in another freezer. It will be collected by an animal incineration company as it does its rounds through the South West. 'Once I saw a giraffe in the back of the van. It was from Longleat,' she tells me. It's a strange, ultra-specialised business, I say. She smiles in agreement: 'But necessary'.

At coffee, I receive condolences from my fellow-volunteers. 'Is it your first loss?' asks Rhi sympathetically.

Access Denied. I arrive for my next shift assuming that I'll be able to visit the release pens to see how the two remaining foxes are faring. But in the intervening week the outside pens have been designated 'staff only'. I can be the one who takes the food in, surely …? 'No. There are badger cubs up there now. Sorry'.

No further explanation is given, and the foxes' notes are missing from the file. For a couple of weeks, the only sign that they are still alive comes via the white board on which their daily rations are written. A snippet about them comes from a member of staff: initially the bowls were turned upside down to prevent birds swooping down to take the food; most foxes work out that they need to lift the bowls to get the food. But the Two Growing Foxes didn't, and one night went without any supper. From then on, the bowls were deposited the right way up in a pragmatic move to ensure that they at least got something.

With summer in full swing and most of the mammals outside, Millie Block is less busy. The main residents are young herring gulls with spotted, fluffy heads; they waddle around the pens in a way that reminds me of pantomime creatures. Of all the animals I've encountered, they seem the least alarmed by the presence of humans and the best able to adapt to life in a confined space. They appear to be enjoying themselves as they potter about their pens, preening and getting in and out of their trays of water. Even this young, they are large birds, and at first I'm nervous of handling them. But I manage to master the technique demonstrated by an experienced volunteer – a swift downwards swoop which pins the wings to the body – sufficiently to box up a group.

It would take too long to catch the fifty older gulls who occupy the largest pen. Their clean involves shooing them up one end while sloshing water over the concrete floor at the other. One large gull spreads his wings to almost their full span, scattering the others around him, and I'm reminded of the power of these birds once full-grown and able to fly. I am even more nervous of cleaning the outside aviary, a task which involves wearing googles to protect my eyes from the resident owls. 'They'll dive at your head,' warns the volunteer briefing me. 'That's how they warn you it's their territory.' Hitchcockian images swirl in my mind. 'Don't look at them,' she advises, adding: 'Are you sure you're okay to do it?' I nod. Wearing a hat and scarf as well as the goggles, I conduct the clean in a submissive manner that is genuinely felt.

Yet Millie Block is not entirely fox-free. One day I look into a pen to see a good-sized young fox sitting in front of the door. His body is taut with vigilance, but he shows no sign of fear and there's yearning in his eyes, a kind of knowing sadness as he returns my gaze. He looks old enough to be outside. I make enquiries and find that his release into an outside pen, planned for that day, has been delayed because of the need for repairs. For the rest of the afternoon I glance in when I pass his pen. Every time he is sitting in the same position, staring longingly at the door.

But the adult fox curled up in a dog bed a few doors down has a very different demeanour. April, one of the resident foxes, in for a few days' treatment for an eye infection caused by a grass seed. The staff had interpreted the howl that had rung through Millie Block when she was first admitted as a a cry of loneliness and taken turns to go and sit with her. Now, despite the confines of her tiled cell, she seems reconciled to her situation. She looks up and blinks in greeting as I go in to clean; one eye is half-closed. I reply verbally; it's a relief to be able to talk to an animal. But almost immediately she puts her head back down to sleep and I mop around her in silence.

When I've finished, I fetch her a treat from the kitchen. It's clear from the smell when I return that she's weed on the clean floor, and there's a curl of poo by the door, possibly by way of reminder that this is her territory. I put the chick on the floor and she comes and gets it, taking it back to her bed to gobble it down, the chicks' feet disappearing into her long jaw. Then she washes her paws and settles back into bed. The sight of all this cosy comfortableness makes the thought of stroking her tempting. I quickly dismiss it: she is an independent creature, not my pet; touching her would seem as much a breach of respect as caressing a human I didn't know well.

Meanwhile, the snack has had a rejuvenating effect. April is looking at me with both eyes fully open, and they sparkle. As she leaves her bed and follows me to the door, I realise I have become a Person of Interest.

At the new monthly meeting aimed at improving communication between staff and volunteers, the chief executive announces a change in policy. A new system to monitor the centre's capacity to care for animals is to be introduced, making it possible to limit admissions for the first time. The people around the table are surprisingly quiet; rumours about the proposed change had been going round and there had been talk of protest. In the emotionally-charged world of animal care, the idea of turning creatures in need away was controversial.

At coffee, I relay the news to a volunteer who had missed the meeting. We both feel the decision is sensible: there are countless orphaned and injured animals in the area served by Secret World, creating a scale of need impossible to meet. The realisation makes her ponder why she volunteers. 'It's a drop in the ocean,' she says. 'It's a little bit of good, I suppose. But I wonder why I'm doing this. Is it for me, or them?'

She answers her own question: 'I think it's fifty-fifty. To give something back – as humans, we do so much damage.' At the same time, she questions how helpful it is to take the birds into hospital: 'Nature didn't mean for us to take them into our care, and we lose quite a lot of them.'

I agree, and shrug, and go back to Millie Block. But a

couple of weeks later, something happens that gives me cause to raise some of the same questions.

I am en route to my shift, part of the early-morning stream of traffic coming into Wells when a crow stalks out into the road in front of me, heading purposefully for the other side. I slow down to give him time to react: surely, like the daft pigeons who parade the streets of London, he'll execute a last minute take-off into the air?

Seconds pass. Wheels turn. Glancing into the rear mirror, I see a black form collapsed at the side of the road. A few feathers float up from the body.

Ever since coming to the wildlife centre I had asked myself what I would do if I found an injured animal by the side of the road. Hitherto my attitude had been a kind of ruthless acceptance: nature is nature; accidents happen. Now, with my new awareness of what is possible, would I join the network of people bundling animals into cardboard boxes and driving them dozens of miles to be taken into human care? I find I am driving on: this is a busy road and it's not easy to stop or turn. I think of the portacabin hospital, so hot and confined, and of the stress of human handling. But if I'm honest, I'm really more motivated by my own concerns - the natural inclination to keep moving, combined with the fact that, as usual, I'm running late.

I'm still debating the matter as I walk onto site. The first person I see is Sarah, the perfect person to grant me absolution for this accidental sin. It happens, she says, and the crow probably died instantaneously.

Soon afterwards, my time as a volunteer comes to an end. Holidays and paid work beckon. Tristan will call me in the autumn when the Two Grown Foxes are ready for release.

THE DAY OF THE FOX

October. I'm working in Bath when Tristan calls. The release site in Devon is ready, and the foxes even more so. 'These are definitely one of the wilder bunches,' he says. The plan is to do a 'soft release', keeping the foxes in an outside pen with daily supplies of food while they get used to their new territory. After a week or two, the door of the pen will be opened and the foxes will be free to roam the wider world.

Ten days later, I drive to Secret World and find Tristan in his van, preparing for the journey to the release site. He's in something of a state, having become so disaffected with his job that he's given in his notice. He will leave in December, as will the chief executive. This will be his last release.

We walk across the site to the pre-release pens. Apart from their nightly deposits of food, the foxes haven't seen humans since the day we found the corpse of Middle Fox. By now they will certainly regard people as predators; catching them may take some time. The big black net Tristan is wielding looks impressive, but it is hard to see how it will stop two determined foxes in their tracks. A second staff member has come to help, and I'm charged with holding the cage and bringing it the right place when necessary.

In the event, it all happens very fast. By dint of simply walking around, the two staff members rout the foxes out of the grass. The larger fox runs up and down the edge of the pen, clearly seeking an exit. But before long, he runs headlong into the net. I run over with the cage and, using a towel, Tristan picks him up by the scruff of the neck and puts him inside. The second fox is captured almost immediately afterwards.

The three of us pause, slightly surprised by the unexpected ease of the process. The foxes in the cage at our feet look fit and healthy, with thick fur that almost glows in the autumn light. The larger fox is strong and stocky, possibly the outcome of a chick-rich diet; he looks back at us with expressionless topaz eyes. The smaller fox huddles behind, taking shelter behind the body of the tougher sibling. We cover the cage with a sheet and carry it to the van.

As we drive down the M5, Tristan talks about the dilemmas and difficulties of his job. This year he has released six groups of foxes, with four or five in each. 'There's no formula for a good release because there are so many factors affecting it,' he says. Different groups behave very differently: some are difficult to catch because they dig tunnels in which they hide, and once a fox died of shock during a catch-up.

Then comes the challenge of finding suitable release sites. Since many people consider foxes to be pests, receptive landowners are a minority. Cultivating relationships with them and negotiating arrangements for release is time-consuming and, even when the perfect plan has been set up, things can go wrong. On one occasion, the owner of a local estate died after a release had been arranged and the son who inherited it gave permission for the local hunt to run by the release site. A lengthy discussion had followed about what to do, and when it was eventually decided to go ahead with the release, there had been outrage from some quarters. Listening, I recognise the strong emotions animals can trigger in people. But most of what I am hearing is a litany of all-too-familiar workplace woes, of being under-paid and under-valued, of insufficient resources for the task at hand, of management failing to understand how things work on the ground.

At Exeter services, we pick up Jess, the prime mover in the foxes' rescue, and her boyfriend. They gasp when they see the fully grown animals in the back of the van. How well they look! How thick and sleek their fur! The van, with its cargo of four humans and two foxes, returns to the M5. Before long we are off the motorway and driving along roads bordered by long, low hills. The release site is on a slope in the foothills of Dartmoor, a narrow slither of land stretching up into woodland. As we pull up on the drive of what was formerly an estate gatehouse, a stout woman in her sixties comes smiling to greet us.

Brenda and her husband have been welcoming foxes on their 11-acre land for years. They have built facilities to host them during the soft release phase, a set of low buildings with an arch-shaped opening onto an outside pen. Overhung with trees and shrubs, the outside section has a moss-covered wooden tunnel in which the foxes can hide. Beyond the wire perimeter the woods beckon enticingly - the foxes will like that - but my main thought is that the new pen is much smaller than the one they've been used to. As we walk back to the van, Brenda tells us that even after release, she puts out chicken wings for the foxes twice a day.

As the person who brought the foxes into human care, Jess is charged with doing the release. She and Tristan take the cage into the building in the enclosure, and deposits it so that the door faces the arch leading to the outside. Then she opens the cage and we watch from behind. Larger Fox shoots straight out and, after a moment's hesitation, bounds through the arch to the outside pen. The other fox stays in the cage.

Back outside, Jess's boyfriend and I position ourselves among the trees with our cameras to watch how things unfold. Larger Fox is running up and down the new enclosure, examining its boundaries and looking up at its corners. After a few moments, it becomes clear that this is more than exploration: there is determination, even desperation, in his ceaseless movements. Every so often he stops and looks at where we, from our places among the vegetation, are looking at him. We decide we are making him anxious and are edging backwards up the slope—

'He's out!' shouts someone. Larger Fox has jumped over one of the corners to the pen and has streaked away into the woods. He has spotted, Brenda tells us ruefully, the weak spot in the pen, the one corner lacking an overhang. Her husband meant to fit one there too, but somehow it didn't happen.

Over tea in the house, a sense of anti-climax prevails. Tristan seems a bit disappointed with the way things have gone; his carefully-laid plans for a staged release have gone awry. The conversation turns to wider fox-related issues. The previous week saw a vote to ban trail hunting on National Trust land narrowly defeated, something which we all feel to be a sign of the organisation's desire to keep pro-hunting landowners sweet. Someone suggests that the way the voting options on the motion, which had come from members but been opposed by the board, were presented had skewed the outcome. Next time, we agree, the pro-fox members will prevail.

Personally, I am pleased with how the day has turned out. I feel a sense of release akin to joy: another orphaned has grown up against the odds and found his freedom.

NOTES

1 I have since read explanations of this behaviour - sometimes known as 'charming' - as both a way of mesmerising prey to make it easier to catch and as a ritual dance associated with courtship. But neither of these explanations work in this context and I am wary of imposing blanket interpretations.

2 Lucy Jones, *Foxes Unearthed: A Story of Love and Loathing in Modern Britain*, Elliott and Thompson, 2016, p 217 ff.

3 James Hillman and Margot McLean, *Dream Animals*, Chronicle Books, 1997, p 13.

4 John Berger, *Why Look at Animals?* Penguin Books, 2009, p 15.

5 Hillman, p 13.

6 David Garnett, *Lady Into Fox and A Man in the Zoo*, The Hogarth Press, 1985.

7 Ibid, p p 83-84.

8 The Animal Welfare Act of 2006 means that caregivers must provide for the five 'welfare needs' of animals. See https://www.rspca.org.uk/whatwedo/endcruelty/changingthelaw/whatwechanged/animalwelfareact

9 Berger, p 15.

10 David Macdonald, in his pioneering study of foxes, records gaping as part of both play and aggressive behaviour. See *Running with the Fox*, Unwin Hyman, 1987, pp 103-4.

ABOUT THE AUTHOR

Dr Alex Klaushofer is an author and journalist who has written extensively on social and affairs and politics in Britain and Middle East. Her work has appeared in publications such as *The Guardian* and *The Daily Telegraph*, along with contributions to BBC radio.

Her books combine reportage, travel writing and one or two other genres. *Paradise Divided* tells the human stories of modern-day Lebanon and explores the mix of social, religious and political forces that make up this complex country.

The Secret Life of God is a kind of spiritual investigation into twenty-first century Britain which chronicles how, in an ostensibly secular age, people are finding new ways of believing and belonging.

Orphaned Foxes is one in a series of short reads – longer than an article but shorter than a book – which explores our relationship to place and nature.

Alex blogs on related subjects at www.alexklaushofer.com.

www.ingramcontent.com/pod-product-compliance
Lightning Source LLC
Chambersburg PA
CBHW020303030426
42336CB00010B/891